Proofreading and Editing

Written by Gunter Schymkiw
Published by World Teachers Press®

Published with the permission of R.I.C. Publications Pty. Ltd.

Copyright © 2000 by Didax, Inc., Rowley, MA 01969. All rights reserved.

First published by R.I.C. Publications Pty. Ltd., Perth, Western Australia. Revised by Didax Educational Resources.

Limited reproduction permission: The publisher grants permission to individual teachers who have purchased this book to reproduce the blackline masters as needed for use with their own students. Reproduction for an entire school or school district or for commercial use is prohibited.

Printed in the United States of America.

Order Number 2-5172
ISBN 1-58324-099-3

C D E F G 08 07 06 05 04

Educational Resources
395 Main Street
Rowley, MA 01969
www.worldteacherspress.com

Foreword

Proofreading and Editing is a series of three blackline master books written to provide students with experience in proofreading and editing written text. A high level of proficiency in these skills is necessary for accurate self-assessment of written work.

Proofreading and Editing – Grades 7-8 consists of a selection of passages that contain punctuation, spelling and grammatical errors. Students are guided through identifying and correcting the errors in each passage. Detailed explanations of more difficult skills such as using direct speech, paragraphing, identifying the features of recount and narrative writing, punctuating playscripts and formatting letters are also included. The choice of topics and humor within the passages makes them appealing to students.

Books in the series are:　　*Proofreading and Editing – Grades 3-4*

　　　　　　　　　　　　　Proofreading and Editing – Grades 5-6

　　　　　　　　　　　　　Proofreading and Editing – Grades 7-8

Contents

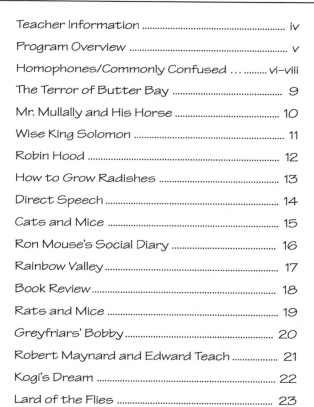

Teacher Information iv

Program Overview v

Homophones/Commonly Confused … .... vi–viii

The Terror of Butter Bay 9

Mr. Mullally and His Horse 10

Wise King Solomon 11

Robin Hood 12

How to Grow Radishes 13

Direct Speech 14

Cats and Mice 15

Ron Mouse's Social Diary 16

Rainbow Valley 17

Book Review 18

Rats and Mice 19

Greyfriars' Bobby 20

Robert Maynard and Edward Teach 21

Kogi's Dream 22

Lard of the Flies 23

Raiko and the Goblin 24

Writing Letters 25

Sammy Cox 26

Factory Farming 27

More Direct Speech 28

Good King Wenceslaus 29

The Eat-A-Bug Cookbook 30

Belling the Cat 31

The Case of the Compound Word … 32

Betty Stuart and "Michi" 33

The Viper Fish 34

Harry de Leyer and the Snowman 35

Splish and Splash 36

Answers 37-40

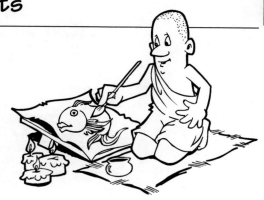

Teacher Information

The activities in this book follow a developmental pattern but can be completed in isolation according to students' individual needs.

A variety of lesson formats can be used in presenting the topics—individual, small-group, or whole-class. Students should be encouraged to contribute in discussions and interact orally with your direction where needed.

Precise instructions telling what has to be done. Forms of punctuation commonly used by students extensively covered.

Clear explanations of new focal points in language that students can understand.

Passage for editing using vocabulary suited to students in Grades 7–8. All sheets are self-contained but allow for extension by you.

Grammar and word study activities.

Usage activities that target common errors in students' writing.

Extension activities to challenge students.

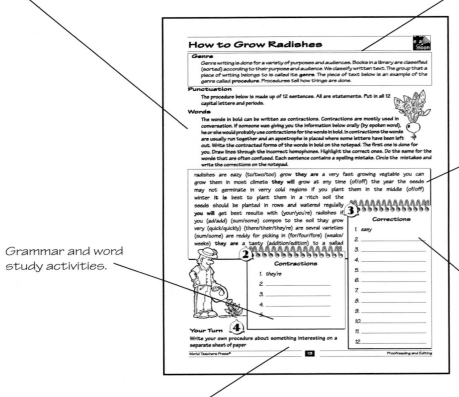

Program Overview

Content Covered	Page Number																								
	9	10	11	12	13	14	15	16	17	18	19	20	21	22	23	24	25	26	27	28	29	30	31	32	33
identifying sentences	●	●	●	●	●	●	●	●	●	●	●	●		●	●	●				●	●	●	●	●	●
identifying questions	●	●	●			●	●	●			●	●			●	●			●	●					
capital letters	●	●	●	●	●	●	●	●	●	●	●	●		●	●	●		●	●	●	●	●	●	●	●
periods	●	●	●	●	●	●	●	●	●	●	●	●		●	●	●				●	●	●	●	●	●
commas	●					●	●				●	●		●	●			●		●	●	●	●	●	●
question marks	●	●	●			●	●				●	●		●	●				●	●					
exclamation marks										●		●			●					●			●	●	
quotation marks						●		●			●									●			●	●	
direct speech						●	●									●				●			●	●	
apostrophes: ownership						●	●	●		●	●	●		●	●	●		●	●		●		●		●
apostrophes: contraction					●	●		●		●	●				●	●		●	●	●			●	●	
hyphens																						●			●
parentheses (brackets)																			●	●					
editing for spelling		●		●	●			●			●				●	●	●	●			●	●			●
common nouns	●	●	●	●																					
proper nouns	●		●	●				●	●	●		●						●							●
compound verbs																		●							
adjectives									●																
verbs		●		●																					
adverbs							●																		
homophones	●	●	●	●	●			●	●	●	●					●		●	●		●	●	●		●
commonly confused	●	●		●	●			●	●	●	●			●		●		●	●		●	●	●		●
compound words																								●	
tautology										●															
paragraphing											●			●											
topic sentences														●											
transition sentences														●											
personal letters																	●								
formal letters																	●								
ambiguity																			●						
play script															●										
exposition										●															
narrative											●		●					●		●			●	●	●
report											●														
procedure					●																				
recount								●																	
drama															●										
discussion																			●						

a / an (22)

"A" and "an" are two forms of the indefinite article. "A" is used before words that begin with consonants: a dog, a house, a tree.

"An" is used before words that begin with vowels: an ant, an egg, an orange.

If the beginning consonant is silent and is followed by a vowel, "an" is used: an hour, an honest mistake.

accept / except (9)

"Accept" means "to agree to receive." Jim accepted the gift gratefully.

"Except" means "all but." Everyone except Jessica got the answer wrong.

ad / add (5)

"Ad" is a shortened slang term for "advertisement."

He is best known for his part in the ad for Boffo Dog Food.

"Add" means to "put together." When you add six to four you get ten.

addition / edition (5)

"Addition" means "the act of adding." The addition of spices made the food more tasty.

An "edition" is one of a number of copies of a book or newspaper.

The story appeared in the morning edition of the newspaper.

air / heir (18)

"Air" means the atmosphere or a gas. The air in the forest was very fresh.

An "heir" is someone entitled to succeed to property or a rank.

Prince Charles is the heir to the British throne.

angels / angles (21)

An "angel" is a spirit. It was as if an angel was protecting him.

An "angle" is a corner. A triangle has three angles.

ate / eight (2)

"Ate" is the past tense of "eat." Jazmin ate her crusts today.

"Eight" is a number. A spider has eight legs.

became / become (21)

"Became" stands alone. "Become" needs a helper (has, have, will).

Jim became sick after eating Mrs. Chiffle's pie. Jim has become sick.

began / begun (16, 18)

"Began" stands alone. "Begun" needs a helper.

Bill began singing loudly. Bill has begun singing.

beside / besides (10)

"Beside" means "next to." The cowboy stood beside his horse.

"Besides" means "apart from." Besides being a good reader, Lily is very good at sports.

best / better (10)

We use "best" when comparing three or more things.

Don Bradman has the best record of all batters in the league.

We use "better" when comparing two things. Colin's score on the test was better than Bo's.

bight / bite (22)

A "bight" is a large curved shoreline.

The Great Australian Bight is part of that continent's southern coastline.

To "bite" is to "grip with the teeth."

"Rover will only bite if you breathe within fifty meters of him," said the proud owner.

blew / blue (9)

"Blew" is the past tense of "blow." The wind blew from the south.

"Blue" is a color. The policeman's uniform is blue.

bought / brought (1, 2, 14, 21, 23)

"Bought" is the past tense of "buy." Tanita bought a beautiful dress at the sale.

"Brought" is the past tense of "bring." Jaimee brought her pet tortoise to school.

To help students remember this, point out the "br" beginnings for "bring" and "brought."

brake / break (23)

A "brake" is a device which slows or stops a vehicle.

The driver put his foot on the brake as he came to the red light.

To "break" means to make inoperable or crack into a number of pieces.

It only took Leonardo two minutes to break his new toy.

came / come (4)

"Came" is the past tense of "come." "Came" never has a helper. Hayley came first in her race. Sometimes "come" has a helper (has, have, had, will).

chased / chaste (16)

"Chased" is the past tense of "chase." The hounds chased the fox.

"Chaste" means "pure" or "decent." The knight was chaste of thought and deed.

desert / dessert (10, 18)

The "desert" is a wasteland. The explorers were lost in the hot, dry desert.

"Dessert" is a sweet course in a meal.

We finished our meal with a dessert of peaches and cream.

did / done (16)

"Did" and "done" are past tense forms of the verb "to do." "Did" stands alone, while "done" requires a helper (has, have).

Genna did her homework. Genna has done her homework.

draw / drawer (1)

"Draw" means "to sketch." Did you draw that lovely picture, Tamara?

A "drawer" is a sliding compartment in a chest. He kept his pencils in a drawer.

eight / ate (See "ate")

except / accept (See "accept")

fair / fare (3)

When we say something is "fair," we mean it is just (it serves justice). Good King Wenceslaus was loved by his people because he was a fair king.

"Fare" is a fee paid for traveling on a bus, train, etc. Loren lost her bus fare.

farther / further (1)

Farther means at or to a greater distance. He went farther down the road. Further means more extended or additional. No further comment.

find / fined (23)

"Find" means to discover by chance. I was lucky to find my watch when it fell in the sand.

"Fined" is the past tense of the verb, "to fine." This means "to impose a penalty (usually money) for some wrongdoing." Vince was fined $100 for stealing.

for / fore / four (5, 23)

"Fore" means "the front part." "Four" is a number. "For" is used in other cases.

He is in the foreground in the picture.

Becky has four parakeets.

This piece of pie is for you. We're bound for South Australia.

forth / fourth (14)

"Forth" is an old word meaning "forward." "Go forth and explore the world," said Mother Pig.

"Fourth" means "in position four." When written 4th, it is called an ordinal number.

Kelly came fourth in her swimming final.

Homophones and Commonly Confused Words

grate / great (21)
A "grate" is a framework of metal bars especially in a fireplace.
The grate was full of glowing coals.
"Great" is an adjective meaning large.
The astronauts of Apollo 11 could see the Great Wall of China from space.

hear / here (4, 23)
You "hear" sounds with your "ear." Did you hear that noise?
"Here" means "in this place." Put your books here.

heard / herd (16)
"Heard" is the past tense of "hear." I heard a strange sound.
"Herd" is a name for a group of animals. A herd of cattle grazed peacefully in the field.

heir / air (See "air")

hole / whole (19)
A "hole" is an opening. The mouse escaped through a hole in the wall.
"Whole" means "complete" or "containing all the parts." Clarence ate the whole pie.

hours / ours (11)
Time is measured in "hours." The plane was four hours late.
"Ours" means "belonging to us." It is a possessive pronoun. That new car in the driveway is ours.

its / it's (10, 11, 21)
"Its" means "belonging to it." It is a possessive pronoun.
The puppy chased its tail.
"It's" is the contracted form of "it is." Do you think it's going to rain?

knew / new (3, 8, 9)
"Knew" is the past tense of "know." Sarah knew all of her multiplication tables.
"New" means freshly made and not used by anyone before. Shaun has some new boots.

knight / night (10)
A "knight" is a high ranking person who has the title "Sir."
Sir Lancelot was one of King Arthur's knights.
"Night" is the period of darkness between sundown and sunrise. We sleep during the night.

know / no (2, 3, 21)
"Know" means "to be aware of something."
Most people know it is bad manners to eat with your elbows on the table.
"No" means "not any" or can be used to deny something.
There are no jellybeans left in the jar. Did you see who took them? No!

laid / lain / lied (14)
"Laid" is the past participle of "lay." It means "put down." The bricklayer laid 500 bricks today.
"Lain" is the past participle of "lie" meaning "to be in a horizontal position." It needs a helper. (has, have)
Mary has lain on her bed. (Note that the past tense of "lie" is also "lay." She lay on the bed.)
"Lied" is the past tense of "lie," meaning "to be untruthful."
During World War I many soldiers lied about their ages so they could join the army.

lay / lie (10, 14)
"Lay" means "to put down or place." Lay your pens on the desk.
"Lie" means "to be in a horizontal position" or "to rest or recline." I'm going to lie on my bed.
Confusion often arises because "lay" is also the past tense of "lie."
The sick child lay in bed groaning.

learn / teach (10)

"Learn" means "to study." I am going to learn the five times table on the weekend.
"Teach" means "to instruct." Today our teacher is going to teach us the five times table.

made / maid (4)
"Made" means "produced." That camera was made in Japan.
A "maid" is a female servant. The maid scrubbed the floor.

meter / meter (11)
A "meter" is a device for measuring something. The man read the electricity meter.
A "meter" is a measurement of length. A meter is made up of one hundred centimeters.

must of / must have (18)
"Must have" is correct usage. Many students say, incorrectly, "must of." This is probably as a result of mishearing the contracted form, "must've."

new / knew (See "knew")

night / knight (See "knight")

of / off (4, 5, 9, 16)
"Of" is a preposition that indicates ownership. She is a relation of mine.
"Off" is a preposition that tells us that something has been removed. He took off his shoes.

peace / piece (2, 21)
"Peace" means calm, quiet or the cessation of war.
The warring tribes decided to make peace.
A "piece" is a "part or portion." May I have a piece of pie please?

picture / pitcher (10)
A "picture" is a drawing, painting, or photograph. A picture hung on the wall.
A "pitcher" is a jug. Joan filled the pitcher with milk.

quick / quickly (5)
"Quick" is an adjective meaning "fast." John is a quick thinker.
"Quickly" is an adverb meaning "rapidly." John thinks quickly.
Sometimes people incorrectly use the adjective as an adverb and vice versa.

quiet / quite (4, 8, 10)
"Quiet" means making little or no noise. The classroom was quiet when the children left.
"Quite" means "to a certain extent." Scott's work is quite good but it could improve.

rain / reign / rein (9)
"Rain" is water that falls from the sky. The rain fell heavily.
The "reign" of a king or queen is the period of their rule.
Shakespeare lived during the reign of Queen Elizabeth I.
A "rein" is used to steer a horse. The jockey pulled the rein so his horse halted.

rote / wrote (8)
If you learn something by "rote" you memorize it by constant repetition without necessarily understanding it.
He learned the poem "The Rime of the Ancient Mariner" by rote.
"Wrote" is the past tense of the verb "to write." He sat down and wrote a long letter.

saw / seen (8, 16, 21)
"Saw" stands alone while "seen" needs a helper (has, have, had).
I saw a flying saucer last night. I have seen a flying saucer once before.

sea / see (8)
The "sea" is a large body of water. The sailor went to sea.
"See" is a verb meaning "to view with the eyes." Did you see that film?

Homophones and Commonly Confused Words

shore / sure (1)
The land along the edge of a sea or lake is the "shore." Robinson Crusoe swam to shore.
"Sure" means "certain." I am sure I've seen that man before.

some / sum (5, 10)
"Some" means "an unspecified number." Some visitors came to our house yesterday.
The "sum" is the "total." The sum of four and five is nine.

tail / tale (10)
An animal has a "tail." The horse brushed flies away with its tail.
A "tale" is a story. "The Little Mermaid" is a fairytale by Hans Christian Andersen.

teach / learn (See "learn")

their / there / they're (1, 2, 4, 5, 8, 9, 11, 18, 21, 22, 23)
"Their" means "belonging to them." That is their house.
"There" is a place. Do you mean the house over there?
"They're" is the contracted form of "they are." Let's see if they're at home.

threw / through (8, 16, 23)
"Threw" is the past tense of "throw." Greg threw the ball back to the catcher.
"Through" is used to indicate starting on one side and finishing on the other.
Little Red Riding Hood walked through the forest and came to her Grandma's house.

tied / tired (21)
"Tied" means "bound." The parcel was neatly tied with string.
"Tired" means "weary." Beau felt very tired after the swimming carnival.

tire / tire (17)
"Tire" means "to grow weary." The teacher began to tire of Leonardo's inattentiveness.
A "tire" is an air-filled tube around a car wheel. He stopped because his tire was flat.

to / too / two (1, 3, 4, 10, 16, 18, 21)
"To" has several meanings and uses. Perhaps it is easiest to remember that it is used in all circumstances where "too" and "two" do not apply.
"Too" is used as an intensifier. This work is too hard. "Too" can mean "also." May I go, too?
"Two" is a number. Birds have two wings.

took / had taken (21)
"Took" stands alone. "Taken" needs a helper (has, have, had). The most common error is when students use the helper (auxiliary) with "took."

warn / worn (1, 23)
"Warn" means "to notify of danger."
The signs on the beach warn us that this is not a safe place to swim.
If something is suffering from wear and tear from constant use, we say it is "worn."
We are getting new carpet at school because the old carpet is worn.

was / were (8, 10)
Both words are past tense forms of the verb "to be." "Was" is singular (used with I, he, she, it).
"Were" is plural (used with you, they). Note that "were" is used with "you" whether it is being used in a singular or plural sense.

waist / waste (1)
Your "waist" is your midriff. The climber tied the rope around his waist.
"Waste" means "what is left over" or "rubbish." Put any waste food in the bin.
"Waste" can also mean "to spend unnecessarily" or "to fail to take advantage of."

The silly boy wasted his money. Do not waste your opportunities.

weather / wether / whether (19)
When we talk about the "weather" we mean the climatic conditions.
On the news the reporter said to expect more rainy weather.
A "wether" is a castrated male sheep. The wether had a wonderful fleece.
"Whether" is used to imply a possibility of choices. Whether you do it or not is up to you.

weak / week (5, 17)
"Weak" means "not strong." The explorers were very weak after so long without food.
A "week" is a period of seven days. It is Hayden's birthday in a week.

were / where (2, 4, 9, 14, 21, 23)
These words are pronounced differently but are often confused in student's spelling. An easy way to stop this confusion is to play an asking game to which the answer is always, "Here!"
Where is your pen? (Student points and answers.) Here!
The teaching point, of course, is that "where" contains its answer, "here."

which / witch (3)
"Which" is used to distinguish a certain member from its group.
"Which book would you like to borrow?" asked the librarian.
A witch is a woman who professes to practice magic. A male witch is a warlock.
Hansel and Gretel came to the cottage of an old witch.

whole / hole (See "hole")

your / you're (5, 10, 16, 17)
"Your" means "belonging to you." That is your pen.
"You're" is the contracted form of "you are." You're on the same team as Colin.

© World Teachers Press® - www.worldteacherspress.com

The Terror of Butter Bay

Sentences

A **sentence** is a group of words that makes sense by itself.
A **statement** is a sentence that gives information.
For example: Bruce went for a swim in Butter Bay.
A **question** is a sentence that asks something.
For example: Why doesn't he go swimming anymore?
All sentences begin with a capital letter. Statements end with a period. Questions end with a question mark.

Words

Nouns are naming words.
Common nouns are the general names for things.
For example: boy, girl, street, country, ship, dog
Proper nouns are special names given to distinguish particular people or things from others in their group.
For example: Ryan, Caroline, Day Street, Australia, Titanic, Scruffy
Homophones are words that sound the same but have different meanings and spellings.

Punctuation

The story below is made up of 13 sentences. There are 12 statements and 1 question. Read the story aloud. If you understand what you are reading you will punctuate it naturally. You normally drop your voice and pause at the end of a sentence. Use different colors for different punctuation marks. The story needs 19 capital letters; 13 to begin sentences and another 6 for proper nouns.

Words

Underline the 2 common nouns and 1 proper noun in the first sentence. Write 8 more common nouns in the story on the notepad.

Draw lines through the incorrect homophones. Circle the correct ones. Do the same for the words that are often confused.

people say a monster lives in butter bay a boy called bruce swam in the surf one day suddenly an arm curled around his (waste/waist) the water began (to/two/too) bubble poor bruce was pulled down the (further/farther) he went the more it hurt he struggled until he was free (to/two/too) lifeguards (brought/bought) him (to/two/too) the (sure/shore) when his mother (bought/brought) him a new pair of swimming trunks she put them in his (draw/drawer) he has never (warn/worn) them he is (to/two/too) scared (to/two/too) swim in butter bay he says it is not safe would you swim (there/their/they're)

Nouns

1. boy
2. _____
3. _____
4. _____
5. _____
6. _____
7. _____
8. _____

Mr. Mullally and His Horse

Punctuation

The story below is made up of 8 sentences.

There are 7 statements and 1 question.

Read the story aloud and listen for the natural pauses.

Punctuate the story by putting in 13 capital letters, 7 periods, 1 question mark and 5 commas.

When three or more things are listed, use a comma to separate all but the last one.

For example: The three little pigs ate onions, garlic, pickles, ginger and jelly.

When reading aloud, these commas indicate slight pauses.

Words

Verbs tell what is done in a sentence.

To find a verb, ask yourself, "What did somebody do in that sentence?"

Underline 5 different verbs in the story.

Each sentence contains a spelling mistake. Circle it and write the correction on the notepad. The first one is done for you.

Draw lines through the incorrect homophones and circle the correct ones. Do the same for the words that are often confused.

mr. mullally ownd a shop on the corner of daisy street evry morning his horse pulled the cart to market mr. mullally (bought/brought) thinges (their/there) (for/ four/fore) his shop he (bought/brought) them back and plased them on the shelves before sunrise do you (no/know) what poeple (bought/brought) at his shop (there/their/they're) (were/where) frutes vegetables candles knives forks spoons and corks mr. mullally allways gave his horse a (piece/peace) of apple the horse (eight/ate) it in a few seckends

Corrections

1. owned   5. _____

2. _____ 6. _____

3. _____ 7. _____

4. _____ 8. _____

Your Turn

Write your own statement or question that contains at least 5 commas. Circle the nouns and underline the verbs.

Wise King Solomon

Punctuation

The story below is made up of 16 sentences. There are 15 statements and 1 question. Read the story aloud and listen for the natural pauses. Punctuate the story by putting in 19 capital letters, 15 periods and 1 question mark.

Words

Draw lines through the incorrect homophones and highlight the correct ones. Proper nouns appear 5 times (some repeated). Underline the proper nouns in the story. List 10 common nouns on the notepad. If you are not sure ask yourself, "Is there such a thing as a … ?"

1

king solomon was a king in israel he lived about three thousand years ago in those days the king was often involved in settling the arguments of ordinary people one day (to/two/too) women came before him they had both recently given birth one of the babies had died each woman claimed the baby that had lived was hers solomon did not (no/know) (which/witch) woman was telling the truth he said he would ask (one/won) of his soldiers (to/two/too) cut the surviving baby in half the first woman agreed that this was (fair/fare) the second woman begged solomon not (to/two/too) do this she said she would rather the other woman had the baby solomon had never intended (to/two/too) cut the baby in half he wanted (to/two/too) find out who the real mother was now he (new/knew) do you (no/know) who the real mother was (to/ two/too)

2

Common Nouns

1. _____ 6. _____
2. _____ 7. _____
3. _____ 8. _____
4. _____ 9. _____
5. _____ 10. _____

Robin Hood

Punctuation

The story below is made up of 15 sentences. All are statements. Put in 34 capital letters and 15 periods.

Words

Draw lines through the incorrect homophones and highlight the correct ones. Do the same for the words that are often confused.

Underline the proper nouns in the story. Some are used more than once.

Color the nouns red and the verbs green in the word wall below the story.

1 Find the 5 spelling mistakes in the sentences listed on the notepad.

prince john lived in england meny years ago his brother was called richard richard went away to fight a war and john became king john was a crule king robin hood was a frend (off/of) richard he went (to/two/too) sherwood forest to get away from john other people joined him (here/hear) (to/two/too) (to/two/too) people who joined robin (were/where) little john and friar tuck while the bad king was on the throne robin and his men robbed rich people who made (there/their/they're) money by taxing the (pour/poor) he gave the money back (to/two/too) the (poor/pour) people robin was (maid/made) an outlaw he and his men loved sherwood forest at nite it was so (quiet/quite) they could (here/hear) a twig if it fell (to/two/too) the ground robin and his men stayed (here/hear) untill the good king returned when richard (came/come) back he made robin and his band of outlaws free men

Nouns and Verbs

2

lived	brother	fight	war	king	went	Sherwood Forest	
joined	throne	robbed	money		taxing	gave	outlaw
loved	twig	fell	ground		stayed		band

Corrections

Sentence 1. ___ ___ ___

Sentence 4. ___ ___ ___ ___

Sentence 5. ___ ___ ___ ___ ___

Sentence 13. ___ ___ ___ ___

Sentence 14. ___ ___ ___ ___

How to Grow Radishes

Genre

Genre writing is done for a variety of purposes and audiences. Books in a library are classified (sorted) according to their purpose and audience. We classify written text. The group that a piece of writing belongs to is called its **genre**. The piece of text below is an example of the genre called **procedure**. Procedures tell how things are done.

Punctuation

The procedure below is made up of 12 sentences. All are statements. Put in all 12 capital letters and periods.

Words

The words in bold can be written as contractions. Contractions are mostly used in conversation. If someone was giving you the information below orally (by spoken word), he or she would probably use contractions for the words in bold. In contractions, the words are usually run together and an apostrophe is placed where some letters have been left out. Write the contracted forms of the words in bold on the notepad. The first one is done for you. Draw lines through the incorrect homophones. Circle the correct ones. Do the same for the words that are often confused. Each sentence contains a spelling mistake. Circle the mistakes and write the corrections on the notepad.

1

radishes are eazy (to/two/too) grow **they are** a very fast growing vegtable you can grow them in most climets **they will** grow at eny time (of/off) the year the seeds may not germinate in verry cold regions if you plant them in the middle (of/off) winter **it is** best to plant them in a ritch soil the seeds should be planted in rows and watered regally **you will** get best results with (your/you're) radishes if you (ad/add) (sum/some) compos to the soil thay grow very (quick/quickly) (there/their/they're) are sevral varieties (sum/some) are reddy for picking in (for/four/fore) (weaks/weeks) **they are** a tasty (addition/edition) to a sallad

2 Contractions

1. they're
2. _____
3. _____
4. _____
5. _____

3 Corrections

1. easy
2. _____
3. _____
4. _____
5. _____
6. _____
7. _____
8. _____
9. _____
10. _____
11. _____
12. _____

4 Your Turn

Write your own procedure about something interesting on a separate sheet of paper.

Direct Speech

Quotation Marks

Sometimes you may want to use the actual words said by a speaker. The words spoken should be enclosed by quotation marks. These can be either single ('…') or double ("…").
We call this form of writing **direct speech**.
Note the punctuation used in the examples of direct speech below.

Speaker First

Caesar yelled, "Ouch!" **Exclamation**
Brutus asked, "Does it hurt very much, Julius?" **Question**
Caesar answered, "It only hurts when I laugh." **Statement**

Speaker Last

"Ouch!" yelled Caesar. **Exclamation**
"Does it hurt very much, Julius?" Brutus asked. **Question**
"It only hurts when I laugh," answered Caesar. **Statement**

Broken Quotation

"Does it," asked Brutus, "hurt very much?"
"It only hurts," answered Caesar, "when I laugh."

Titles

When a speaker includes the title of a book, film, etc., this must be enclosed in quotation marks. Single and double quotation marks should be used alternately in such cases.
"I've just seen a film called 'Sodgilla,' " said Malcolm.

Punctuation

Punctuate the dialogues below using the above information as a model.

"Rockjaw" needs 6 sets of quotation marks, 12 capital letters, 2 apostrophes, 2 commas, 2 question marks, 5 periods and 1 exclamation point.

"The Test" needs 6 sets of quotation marks, 10 capital letters, 2 apostrophes, 1 question mark, 6 commas, 1 exclamation point and 4 periods.

A new line has already been taken for each new speaker.

 Whenever a new speaker talks, a new line should be taken.
Remember—a new speaker, new line!

 Rockjaw

ive just been to see a movie called rockjaw said terry

what was it about asked mavis

its about a boxer called rockjaw replied terry

was it good asked raelene

sensational exclaimed terry

 The Test

mother asked are you reading another goosepimples book colin

colin answered im studying for tomorrows test

his little sister shouted you are not

we have to said colin in a calm voice write a report about our favorite book

Cats and Mice

Punctuation

The story below is made up of 17 sentences. It needs 23 capital letters, 17 periods, 4 sets of quotation marks, 4 commas, 1 question mark and 2 apostrophes showing ownership. Use different colors to put them in.

Words

Adverbs make our writing more interesting. They add to verbs and tell how something is done. They often end in **ly**. For example: The children played **happily**. "Happily" is the adverb. It tells how the children played. There are 5 adverbs ending in **ly** in the story. Highlight them, write them on the notepad and explain how they add meaning to their verbs.

1

a long time ago cats and mice liked each other a cat would lift its paw and wave if it saw a mouse mice would bow politely when they saw a cat one morning the king of cats was walking in the forest as he was walking his claw became stuck in a hunters net he bawled out loudly some mice heard him calling they came quickly my claw is stuck he called angrily can you gnaw the string in this net and set me free he asked we are running late for a party on mrs. squeaks lawn said one mouse
she makes the nicest strawberry jam said another licking his lips hungrily
the mice went off the king of cats got free but he was very angry he made a law if a cat saw a mouse it was its duty to try to catch it that is why cats and mice are no longer friends

In some titles, minor words don't begin with capitals.
For example: King **of** Spain.

Did you notice that a new line was taken for a new speaker?
Try to remember this in your own writing.

2

Adverbs

1. _____ _____

2. _____ _____

3. _____ _____

4. _____ _____

5. _____ _____

Ron Mouse's Social Diary

- The passage below is an example of the **recount** genre.
  A **recount** is a piece of writing which tells a series of events in the order in which they happened.
- Capital letters are used for proper nouns. The name of a restaurant and film are used in the recount below; don't forget the capitals.
- Titles of books, films and poems are also enclosed in quotation marks. Quotation marks are usually seen enclosing the actual words someone says.
- Ron begins his account of each day the same way, "On … day …" This is not good writing. Try to vary your sentences.

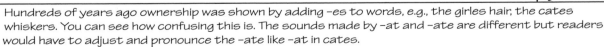

Info… Hundreds of years ago ownership was shown by adding –es to words, e.g., the girles hair, the cates whiskers. You can see how confusing this is. The sounds made by –at and –ate are different but readers would have to adjust and pronounce the –ate like –at in cates.
This changed to "s." Just as in contractions, the apostrophe reminds us that something has been left out.
To show ownership, write the owner, place an apostrophe after the owner, then add –s if it is normally said.
Example: the eggs of the chicken—the chicken's eggs; the eggs of the chickens—the chickens' eggs

Punctuation

1 The passage below is made up of 15 sentences. It needs 49 capital letters, 16 periods, 5 apostrophes (4 in contractions and 1 showing ownership).

Words

Draw lines through the incorrect homophones and circle the correct ones. Do the same for the words that are often confused. Each sentence contains a spelling mistake. Circle the mistakes and write the corrections on the notepad.

on munday i (was/were) dining at terrys house of fine food id reely recommend the food (there/their) on tuseday i ran (in to/into) clint westwood julia robots and jim curry i didnt (sea/see) the stop sine it was all sorted out down at the police stashon on wensday i went to the movies i (saw/seen) a film called people doing silly things to eatch other this is a comedy you hafto (see/sea) its a laf a second on thurday i was playing with my poodle in the park i pickt up a stick and (threw/ through) it for him to fetch just as i looked up i (saw/seen) the basketball champoin called jumping jordan shooting hoops i went over (there/their/they're) to arsk for his autograph it was when he pickt me up and stuck me in the hoop i (new/knew) id upset him on friday someone came with a ladda to get me down on saturday i went to the office where it was nice and (quiet/quite) and (rote/wrote) this collum

2 ### Corrections

1. *Monday*
2. _____
3. _____
4. _____
5. _____
6. _____
7. _____
8. _____
9. _____
10. _____
11. _____
12. _____
13. _____
14. _____
15. _____
16. _____

3 **Your Turn** Write an account of your week.

Rainbow Valley

Adjectives

Adjectives are words used to add meaning to nouns. Using adjectives can make your stories more interesting to readers. There are a number of different types of adjectives.

Descriptive adjectives tell "what sort." Examples: the **yellow** flower; the **little** girls; the **sad** clown

Numerical adjectives describe "the amount of."
They can be **definite**. Examples: **three** girls ; **two hundred** children
They can be **indefinite**. Examples: **several** boys; **many** children; **any** color; bubbles **galore**

Demonstrative adjectives can be thought of as "pointing words."
Examples: **this** car; **those** apples; **that** elephant

Interrogative adjectives are used to ask questions. Examples: **which** film; **what** type

Distributive adjectives tell "which members of a group." Example: **every** child in the class

Compound adjectives are made up of two or more words. They are joined by hyphens.
Examples: a **loose-fitting** shirt; a **dot-to-dot** book

Punctuation

The story below is made up of 14 sentences. It needs 19 capital letters and 14 periods. Put them in.

Words

It contains 25 adjectives (note White Cat Town is a proper noun). Highlight one adjective from each sentence and write it on the notepad. Draw lines through the incorrect homophones and circle the correct ones. Do the same for the words that are often confused. Use a different color to that used for highlighting the adjectives.

1

rainbow valley is a colorful place tourists go (there/their/they're) every year and marvel at the unusual things they see pink elephants (wonder/wander) down the well-lit streets people there have green dogs cats can be any color (except/accept) white white cats are caught in the winter when they can be easily seen in the black snow they are taken to the pretty village called white cat town the purple people living there are proud (off/of) the valley they have gray hair rainbow valley has beautiful gardens and each house has a rich lawn of [blew/blue] grass the mayor is a pleasant happy man we (were/where) there on a recent visit and he was opening a (new/knew) building suddenly the green sky turned yellow it (began/begun) to (rain/rein/reign) huge drops of delicious red jelly

2

Adjectives

(Sentence 1)	colorful
(Sentence 2)	_____
(Sentence 3)	_____
(Sentence 4)	_____
(Sentence 5)	_____
(Sentence 6)	_____
(Sentence 7)	_____
(Sentence 8)	_____
(Sentence 9)	_____
(Sentence 10)	_____
(Sentence 11)	_____
(Sentence 12)	_____
(Sentence 13)	_____
(Sentence 14)	_____

Genre

The piece of writing below is an example of the **exposition** genre. An exposition provides information favoring a particular point of view. Advertisements, newspaper editorials, book reviews and speeches are all examples of the exposition genre.

Exclamation Points

Exclamations are used to show strong feelings such as fear, anger, or surprise. An exclamation point at the end tells the reader that what is written is to be expressed forcefully. For example: Help! Stop it!

Tautology

Tautology is the needless repetition of an idea in a sentence. For example: Jack looked up and saw a **big giant.**

Punctuation

The exposition below is made up of 16 sentences. There are 13 statements, 2 exclamations and one question. Punctuate the sentences and add capital letters. Tautology has been used in sentences 1, 3, 9 and 12. Draw lines through the unnecessary words in these sentences.

Info... Proper nouns: Words in the titles of books or stories begin with capital letters and the titles are enclosed in quotation marks.

Remember this when punctuating sentences 2 and 5. The passage needs 3 additional apostrophes. One is an apostrophe showing ownership and the other 2 are in contractions.

Words

Draw lines through the incorrect homophones and circle the correct ones. Do the same for the words that are often confused. Sentence 14 contains too much information. Cross out some of it out so it is easier to understand.

ive just finished reading a very unique book (it's/its) called strange (tales/tails) and is written by ron mouse the book is full of true facts it can (teach/learn) you a lot my favorite (tale/tail) in the book is called silent (knight/night) ron tells how he fell (to sleep/asleep) when he (was/were) at the south pole and woke up (beside/besides) a polar bear imagine that (beside/besides) being very interesting it has (some/sum) wonderful (pictures/pitchers) ron himself is in most of them this is rons second book his other book tells of his adventures in the (desert/dessert) of both the (to/two/too) books i think this is the (best/better) the book is (quite/quiet) expensive because (its/it's) cover is made of yak leather (its/it's) the sort of book youd be pleased to (lie/lay) down with and read or (lie/lay) on (your/you're) coffee table near the mantelpiece under the moose antlers on the wall to impress the neighbors what more can i say go out and (by/buy/bye) a copy now

Unfortunately, Ron's book contains some untrue "facts." What is wrong with his polar bear story?

_____

_____

Rats and Mice

Genre

The piece of writing below is an example of the information report genre. An information report presents factual information about a class of things. For example: rats, comets, ancient civilizations.

Paragraphs

The report below is arranged in **paragraphs**. A paragraph is usually made up of a number of sentences about the same topic. Sometimes a single sentence can be a paragraph.

The paragraphs of an information report are usually organized as follows:

(a) a beginning that introduces the topic;
(b) factual information; and
(c) general concluding comments.

Commas

Commas are used when additional information that is not essential to the meaning of the sentence is added.

Example 1: Jazmin, the little girl who sits next to Colin, is an excellent student.

The main information in this sentence is that Jazmin is an excellent student.

Example 2: The students in Mr. Nutter's class are excellent students.

In this sentence the information that the students are in Mr. Nutter's class **is** essential to the meaning so commas are not used.

Quotations

Quotations should be enclosed in quotation marks.

For example: The camel is known as "the ship of the desert."

Note that the period here is placed inside the last quotation mark.

Punctuation

The information report below is made up of 18 sentences. There are 17 statements and 1 question. Punctuate the report with capital letters and periods. Sentences 6 and 14 both require 2 commas. A comma is needed in sentence 11. Quotation marks are needed in sentence 17. Two apostrophes are needed.

Words

Circle the spelling mistake in each sentence. Write the corrections neatly above each word. Draw lines through the incorrect homophones or words that are often confused. Circle the correct words.

rats and mice can be found in all parts of the werld people have been trying to protect themselfs from these small mammals since history was first recorded they are mentioned in writings from anchent egypt

getting rid of them is not an easy tarsk some femail rats can have up to eighty young in a year like cats (there/their/they're) enemys rats land on (there/their/ they're) feet when they fall they can servive a fall of twenty meters without being injured rats have been known to tred water for seventy-two (hours/ours)

rats and mice find peoples houses comftable they eat most foods that we licke they spred such diseases as plague typhus and salmonella youve all seen a cat scraping (its/it's) nales on wood (its/it's) doing this to keap them from growing too long rats and mice their partners in crime have the same problem with their teath they hafto chew on things to keep them the right length sometimes they cause fires by chewing on elecktric wires rats and mice have been (known/no-one) as lapdogs of the devel can you understan why

Greyfriars Bobby

Genre

The piece of writing below is an example of the **narrative** genre. A narrative text is an account of events or experiences. Novels or short stories are examples of **fictional narratives**.

The passage below tells of events that actually took place. It is an example of **factual narrative**.

Apostrophes

The apostrophe of possession (ownership) is often not used in the names of places or landmarks.

For example: Princes Highway; Queens Road; Kings Cross; Greens Beach; St. Huberts Island

Proper Nouns

Proper nouns involving the use of a place name as well as a general word usually start with a capital letter for the place name and a small letter for the general word.

For example: Afghan hound; Skye terrier; Siamese cat; African violet; French fries

Punctuation

The factual narrative below is made up of 12 statements and one exclamation. Commas enclosing information that is not essential are needed in sentences 2, 3 and 7. Six apostrophes that show ownership are needed. Put in all punctuation corrections.

1.

john gray was a policeman he lived in scotlands capital city edinburgh johns dog bobby loved him very much bobby was a little skye terrier he used to accompany john on his patrols john died and was buried in the yard of greyfriars church for fourteen years bobby his faithful friend stayed by his masters grave what a loving friend he was edinburghs people came to love the little dog they made sure he always had enough to eat bobby died in 1872 a statue of john grays faithful friend was made it still stands today

2.

Match the endings with their beginnings. Use a dictionary to help you. Write a definition for each word on the back of this sheet or on a separate sheet of paper.

measles, onion, stew, toast, devil, chop suey, checkers, rope trick, dressing, cheese

1. Indian _____

2. Spanish _____

3. Greek _____

4. Irish _____

5. American _____

6. Tasmanian _____

7. German _____

8. Swiss _____

9. French _____

10. Chinese _____

Robert Maynard and Edward Teach

Punctuation

The article below is made up of 17 sentences. It needs 30 capital letters, 17 periods, 3 sets of quotation marks, 4 commas and 4 apostrophes (3 showing ownership and 1 used in a contraction).

Words

Each sentence has a word either misspelled or used incorrectly. Highlight each of these words then write the corrections on the notepad.

Notice that italics have been used to write the name of Maynard's ship, *The Pearl*.

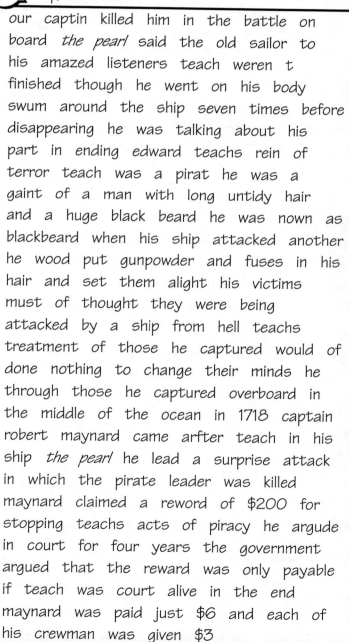

our captin killed him in the battle on board *the pearl* said the old sailor to his amazed listeners teach weren t finished though he went on his body swum around the ship seven times before disappearing he was talking about his part in ending edward teachs rein of terror teach was a pirat he was a gaint of a man with long untidy hair and a huge black beard he was nown as blackbeard when his ship attacked another he wood put gunpowder and fuses in his hair and set them alight his victims must of thought they were being attacked by a ship from hell teachs treatment of those he captured would of done nothing to change their minds he through those he captured overboard in the middle of the ocean in 1718 captain robert maynard came arfter teach in his ship *the pearl* he lead a surprise attack in which the pirate leader was killed maynard claimed a reword of $200 for stopping teachs acts of piracy he argude in court for four years the government argued that the reward was only payable if teach was court alive in the end maynard was paid just $6 and each of his crewman was given $3

Corrections

1. _____
2. _____
3. _____
4. _____
5. _____
6. _____
7. _____
8. _____
9. _____
10. _____
11. _____
12. _____
13. _____
14. _____
15. _____
16. _____
17. _____

Kogi's Dream

Genre

The piece of writing below is an example of the **fictional narrative** genre.

Paragraphs

The story is written in paragraphs. A **paragraph** is usually made up of a number of sentences about one event or idea in a story.

You must start a new line when beginning a new paragraph.

The **topic sentence** of a paragraph tells what the main idea of the paragraph is. It is usually located at the beginning of the paragraph.

Transition sentences link one paragraph to the next. They give some idea of what the next paragraph is about without developing the idea fully.

Punctuation

The story below is made up of 19 sentences. Put in all punctuation.

Non-essential word commas are needed in sentences 1, 6, 10, 15 and 16.

Three apostrophes of possession are needed.

Words and Sentences

Cross out the incorrect words in the parentheses and circle the correct ones.
Use 2 different colors to highlight the **topic sentences** and **transition sentences.**

Info...

Notice that new lines are started for new paragraphs.

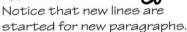

kogi a priest lived in japan over a thousand years ago he loved to paint pictures of trees flowers birds and animals he liked painting pictures of fish most of all

he was painting a picture of a fish one day and began to feel sick he went to his bed to (lay/lie) down two young priests koichi and hidesato came to visit him kogi did not move they thought he was dead kogis body was (laid/lain/lied) on a bed in the temple koichi and hidesato his two young pupils sat by the body for three days

on the (forth/fourth) morning they were shocked to see kogi open (his/he's) eyes he told them that he had been turned into a fish in the water he saw some food on the line he ate it and felt himself being pulled out of the water he found himself in the boat of his friend bunshi

bunshi a fisherman sold him to juro kogi said that he had woken in the temple just as juros knife came down on him

the two young priests ran (strait/straight) to juros house juro and his family (were/where) just sitting down to eat a large fish that he had (bought/brought) from bunshi

Lard of the Flies

Genre

A **play script** belongs to the genre known as **drama**. It usually begins with a list of characters and a setting called the **scene**. In longer plays, there can be a number of scene changes. Characters' **names** are usually written in **capitals**. If it is written to be acted there will usually be **directions** for actors to follow, generally enclosed in parentheses. Some plays, such as radio plays, are written just to be read aloud. Even so, they contain directions about sound effects. When writing a drama on a word processor, the directions are often written in **italics** so actors can easily distinguish **directions** from **dialogue**. Film scripts also contain special camera instructions such as CU (close up) or LS (long shot).

Info... Notice how a colon (:) is used to separate the character from the dialogue. Also note that quotation marks are not used in a play script format.

People being addressed are always separated from the rest of the sentence with commas. For example: Peggy, please get on with your work.

Get on with your work please, Peggy.

Please, Peggy, get on with your work.

Exclamation marks are probably used more often in this type of writing than any other. Decide where you want to use them.

Punctuation

Punctuate the drama below. Choose 2 different colors to highlight the different characters. Use another color to highlight any directions. You do not have to change the punctuation for the directions. Characters: Brian Blowfly, Bruce Housefly.

SCENE: the local dump

BRUCE HOUSEFLY (shouting): brian blowfly ive got good news

BRIAN BLOWFLY (looking up): hurry up ive got a date with a doll at mr browns bin

BRUCE (excitedly): this is big

BRIAN (becoming annoyed): get to the point

BRUCE: you know that old bookshop on the corner

BRIAN: you mean old mr winkles place

BRUCE: thats the one theyre pulling it down and putting up a fast food place

BRIAN: wow some free grease

BRUCE: no more five kilometer flights to the dump

BRIAN: ill miss old mr winkle a bit

BRUCE: i wont he rolled up a copy of the saturday evening pest and splattered my cousin with it last week

BRIAN: thats bad

BRUCE: its not so bad none of the family liked him much

BRIAN: thanks for the tip

BRUCE: dont mention it

(They buzz off stage)

Raiko and the Goblin

Words

Each sentence in the story below contains a spelling mistake or a word used incorrectly. Circle the mistake and write the correction above in the space provided.

Punctuation

Where you see (P) written after a sentence, add any punctuation that is needed within the sentence.

Sentences labeled (PS) contain direct speech. Punctuate these sentences with quotation marks as well.

Raiko were a rich man. He lived in japan hundreds of years a go. (P) Even through he was rich, he wasnt happy. (P) Every minute off his day was spent worrying about his money. He worried that someone would steal it off him. High above Raikos village was a moutain. (P) On that mountain their lived a goblin. He wasnt happy with what he seen. (P) He saw raiko sitting a lone in his counting house. (P) He could read Raikos thoughts as he sits counting his money. (P) Raiko had a plan to safe himself money. Years earlier his father had build beautiful gardens. They was his way of thanking the people of the village. His planning and there hard work had made him a rich man. Raiko had disided to dismiss the gardeners. The gardens brung him no money, so why should he pay (P) men to look after them (P) As he made these plans Raiko begun to feel sick He lied on his bed and groaned. All of a suddenly he saw an old priest standing nearby.

what do you want askt raiko (PS)

the stranger answered i want you to take better care of the people of you're village (PS)

Raiko was inraged. He picked up a dagger and through it at the stranger. The old priest jumped a side. Raiko could not beleive what he saw next. The old man in the doorway had turned into a huge spidder. Two of raikos gardeners came running when they herd his screams. (P) They chaste the monster to a cave in the mountain. it stopped and said tell your master to used his money to help the poor people of the village (PS)

Raiko thanked them when they return. Raiko spended half of his fortune to help the poor villagers. To his surprise, although he had less money, Raiko was much more happier. When the goblin looked down on the valley and saw the happy villagers it made him happy to.

Writing Letters

Letters can be put into two main categories.
Personal letters are those written to someone well known to the writer.
Formal letters (sometimes called business letters) are those written to someone not known personally to the writer.

Personal Letter

Study the format of the personal letter below. Circle the errors and write the corrections on the notepad.

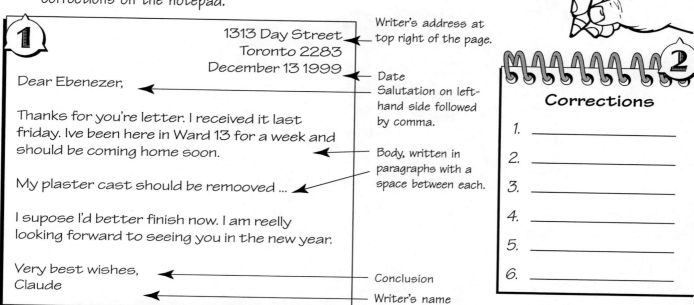

1

1313 Day Street
Toronto 2283
December 13 1999

Writer's address at top right of the page.

Date

Dear Ebenezer,

Salutation on left-hand side followed by comma.

Thanks for you're letter. I received it last friday. Ive been here in Ward 13 for a week and should be coming home soon.

My plaster cast should be remooved ...

Body, written in paragraphs with a space between each.

I supose I'd better finish now. I am reelly looking forward to seeing you in the new year.

Very best wishes,
Claude

Conclusion

Writer's name

2 Corrections

1. _____
2. _____
3. _____
4. _____
5. _____
6. _____

Formal Letter

Study the format of the formal letter below. Circle the errors and write the corrections on the notepad.

3

1314 Day Street
Toronto 2283

Writer's address at top right of the page.

December 13 1999

Date

Morton Gumber
Editor
The Daily Mail
BOSTON, MA

Name, position or title and address of person being written to.

Dear Mr Gumber,

Salutation

As a long-time reader of your newspapper I'd like to comment on the type of letters being published. Im sick and tyred of reading the same carping, whining letters from people who write to you. Only last weak ...
If this trend continues I shall be canceling my subscrishen. In conclusion, I would appreciate it if more positive letters was printed.

Body, written in paragraphs with a space between each.

Yours sincerely,

Conclusion
Space for handwritten signature

M. Purvis

Mervyn Purvis

Writer's name

4 Corrections

1. _____
2. _____
3. _____
4. _____
5. _____
6. _____

Sammy Cox

Words

Each sentence in the factual narrative below contains a spelling mistake or a word incorrectly used. Put a ring around each mistake and write corrections on the lines provided.

Punctuation

Where you see (P) written after a sentence add any missing punctuation.

1. Sammy Coxs father loved too go hunting. (P) _____
2. He was killed in a hunting axedent when sammy was still very young. (P) _____
3. Sammys uncel took care of the young boy. (P) _____
4. In 1789 he took Sammy on a waling trip. _____
5. They made the long trip from Ingland to Tasmania. _____
6. The sailors on the ship like playing tricks on the sixteen-year-old boy. _____
7. They said his uncle was going to abandon him on a desserted island. _____
8. These story's frightened young sammy. (P) _____
9. He hide in the bush. _____
10. He was so afraid he didnt come out of hiding when his uncle and the crew call for him. (P) _____
11. When they werent able to find him, they thought he must of had a dreadful accident. (P) _____
12. They sailed a way, leaving poor sammy behind. (P) _____
13. Sammy made freinds with the local Aboriginal people. _____
14. He lived amongst them until 1806. _____
15. In that year an english settlement begun in Launceston. (P)_____
16. Sammy worked for a famley called cox. (P) _____
17. He even took on there name. _____
18. When he died in 1891 he was 118 years of old. (P-2 commas) _____
19. Sammy has lived humbly all of his life. _____
20. When he died however it was found that his uncle was been a very rich man. (P-2 commas) _____
21. Sammy had been the missing air to his fortune.
_____

Compound Verbs

Sometimes verbs are made up of more than one word. The dog **has run** across the road.
Such verbs are known as **compound verbs**.
Highlight the compound verbs in sentences 2, 7, 19, 20 and 21.

> **Notice** that sentences 18 and 20 both begin "When he died ..."
> This is not good writing. It is important to vary sentence beginnings. Often we don't notice these things when writing a first draft. As you read through a first draft pay attention to your sentence beginnings to ensure that there is some variety.
> Cross out the second "When he died ..." and write a different beginning.

Factory Farming

Genre

The piece of writing below is an example of the **discussion** genre. In a discussion, various points of view are examined. It can conclude with a recommendation based on material presented.

Words

Each sentence in the **discussion** below contains a spelling mistake or a word incorrectly used. Circle the mistakes and write corrections on the lines provided. If you see (L) after a sentence it means some words have to be left out. Draw lines through the unnecessary words.

Punctuation

1 Add any missing punctuation where you see (P) written after a sentence.

The worlds poplation is growing rapidly. (P) _____ There are more people than at any other time in histry. _____ All of them people have to be fed. _____ People have developed very efficient ways to growing food. _____ Some people say that some of the methods used are crule. _____ Should they be out lawed (P) _____ What do youse think (P) _____ Do you like eaten chicken (P) _____

In australia most hens is raised in the huge sheds. (PL) _____ This is call battery farming. _____ Hens raised in these sheds may spend their hole lives inside. _____ They only have a small space in which to move in. (L) _____ Some hens cages have slopey wire floors. (P) _____ The floors slope so the eggs can roll down to be collection. _____ This type of farming reducts the price of chicken products. _____ Would you like to pay $1 for a egg (P) _____ Some chickens say chickens get used to living in these cages. _____ People must decide weather they are for battery farming or against it. _____ There is a way to stop this method from farming. _____ Dont by things grown on battery farms. (P) _____

Ambiguity

2

Sometimes what is written can be understood in a number of different ways. We say that such writing is **ambiguous**. Usually punctuation can be used to correct ambiguity. Rewrite these sentences correctly on the back of this sheet.

(a) "When do we eat Bill?" asked the hungry cowboys. (Add a comma so it is clear that the cowboys don't want to eat a person called Bill.)

(b) That girl called Colin is my sister. (Add 2 sets of quotation marks and 2 commas.)

(c) Did you lay that egg on the table? (Change a word.)

(d) Last night some people were evacuated from a burning building by firemen still in their pajamas. (Rewrite so it is clear that the people evacuated were the ones in their pyjamas.)

(e) He raised fatter pigs than his father. (Think of a better way of writing this.)

More Direct Speech

Abbreviations – Initials

Initials are followed by periods.

For example: W.C. Fields was a comic actor of early films.

Parentheses

Parentheses, which are also known as **round brackets**, have several uses.

They can be used to include additional information.

For example: The whale was the length of a basketball pass (about 20 meters).

They can be used to show that singular or plural words may be used.

For example: The cost of entry is one dollar bill per child. Parents are asked to enclose the bill(s) in the envelope provided.

They can be used to indicate the years of birth and death.

For example: Wyatt Earp (1848–1929) is the most famous lawman of America's West.

Nicknames are often enclosed in quotation marks.

For example: Jack Dempsey, the famous boxer, was known as the "Manassa Mauler."

With increased use of word processors, these names are now often shown bold or italics.

Punctuation

Punctuate the factual narrative passage below. There are 10 examples of direct speech. Remember to use quotation marks and parentheses when necessary.

Notice how a new line is started for each new speaker.

Nationalities such as Australians and Englishmen are proper nouns and begin with capitals.

f r spofforth 1853–1926 was an australian cricketer he was a fast bowler he had the nickname the Demon spofforth played for club sides in england when he wasnt representing australia in test matches on one occasion he was unhappy after some catches were dropped off his bowling f r d monroe was his team-mate he told the Demon to cheer up

in australia he said even your wonderful australians missed some catches off your bowling

never exclaimed spofforth i coached them

what did you do asked monroe

he answered in the part of australia that i come from weve got hedgerows

go on said monroe

on sundays i used to take a packet of stones from my pocket said spofforth

then what asked the englishman

i walked on one side of the hedges and they walked on the other continued spofforth

how did you improve their catching asked his curious friend

i threw the stones into the hedges and they caught the sparrows as they came out said the demon

Good King Wenceslaus

Capital Letters

Capital Letters are used for words associated with gods, religions, or positions of high rank. For example: Our Father Who art in heaven, hallowed be Thy name ..., Christianity, Christians, Buddhism, Buddhist, Islam, Moslem, Hindu, Hinduism, Queen Elizabeth, Mary Queen of Scots, the Prince of Wales, President Lincoln, Prime Minister Menzies.

Info...

Note that paganism is a general term for religions other than Christianity, Judaism or Islam. It does not begin with a capital, nor do words deriving from it such as "pagan."

Punctuation

Add the corrections in the parentheses to each sentence below. Add any periods that are needed.

1

king wenceslaus 903–935 was king of bohemia over a thousand years ago (1 set of parentheses, 4 capitals) bohemia was part of the country we now (no/know) as the czech republic (3 capitals) wenceslaus had a twin brother called boleslaus (2 capitals) (there/their/they're) mother drahomira was a pagan (2 capitals, 2 commas) wenceslaus was (brought/bought) up by his grandmother ludmilla (2 capitals, 1 comma) she was a christian (2 capitals) drahomira the (to/two/too) boys mother (bought/brought) boleslaus up as a pagan (2 capitals, 2 commas, 1 apostrophe of ownership) she hated christians and had ludmilla killed (3 capitals) wenceslaus gathered an army and (fought/fort) the pagans (1 capital) he (won/one) a (great/grate) battle (1 capital) his soldiers said that they (saw/seen) (to/two/too) (angles/angels) looking over

Words

Draw lines through the incorrect homophones or words that are often confused. Highlight the correct ones.

2

Find Out

Which feast did Good King Wenceslaus look upon?

_____

_____

wenceslaus during the conflict (2 capitals) wenceslaus mother asked him to come to the city of bunzlau to have (piece/peace) talks (1 apostrophe of ownership, 2 capitals) when he arrived boleslaus his pagan brother murdered him (2 commas, 2 capitals) the people of bohemia (were/where) horrified by what had (took/taken) place and turned to christianity (3 capitals) boleslaus repented and (became/become) a christian (2 capitals) he had wenceslaus body buried in the capital city prague (3 capitals, 1 apostrophe of ownership, 1 comma)

The Eat-A-Bug Cookbook

Hyphens

Hyphens are used in a number of ways. Sometimes their use is optional.
Compound Words involving letters and nouns are hyphenated. For example: X-ray; T-bone steak; U-turn
The title "Eat-A-Bug" is hyphenated because the writer wants this invented term to be run together as if it were one word.
When the words **self** and **well** are part of an adjective, a hyphen is used. For example: a well-known writer; a self-centred person
Hyphens can be used to mean "up to and including." For example: the 1914–18 War

Punctuation

1

Punctuate the passage below.

are you tied of eating the same old thing do you long for the taste of something really diffrent david george gordon a us auther has written a book that may help you (it's/its) titel is The Eat-A-Bug Cookbook in the book (there/their/they're) are recepes which include such treats as spiders ants centipedes silkworms and grasshoppers

in (a/an) interview gordon said after people have a (bite/bight) they are usualy surprised the bible he said tells us that john the baptist lived on a diet of locusts and hunny

louis armstrong a famous musician drank a mixture made of boiled cockrochs to cure a (saw/sore) throat gordon says i like to point out that everythink has a reason for being

other (sauces/sources) riport that tarantulas taste like crab to cook them (there/their/they're) legs are (tied/tired) back before (there/their/

Words

Each sentence has one spelling mistake. Circle the error and write corrections on the notepad. Cross out the incorrect words in the parentheses and circle the correct ones.

they're) throwen on hot coals termites are verry rich in (ion/iron)

i (wonder/wander) how long it will be before people will be bying them at the local grocery store purhpas it will be sooner than you think

Corrections

2

1. _____
2. _____
3. _____
4. _____
5. _____
6. _____
7. _____
8. _____
9. _____
10. _____
11. _____
12. _____
13. _____
14. _____

© World Teachers Press® - www.worldteacherspress.com

Belling the Cat

Punctuation

The fictional narrative below is made up of 20 sentences. It needs 23 capital letters, 18 periods and one exclamation point. Seven apostrophes are needed—4 in contractions and 3 to show ownership. Ten sets of quotation marks are needed. There are 4 sets of broken quotations. You must add 12 additional commas. Most of these are associated with direct speech but 2 are needed for inserted words.

Words

Each sentence contains an incorrect word. Some have been spelled incorrectly, while others are used incorrectly. Circle the words then write the corrections on the notepad.

the mice of a certain household were going threw difficult times mr and mrs roseworthys old cat had dyed and theyd bought a new one for the last four years the old cat hadnt warried them very much

the new cat however was a teror to the mice population hed only been their for a week and had caught ten mice already somethink had to be done quickly they decided to held a meeting to discuss the problem

my brothers said one of there leaders this house isnt a safe place for mice since the old cat died

1

Info... Notice where new paragraphs have been started and new lines have been started for new speakers.

another joint in saying we have to do something before we are wiped out

the problem is said the first mouse that we can not here the cat because he sneaks up so quietly we need to find some way to worn us he is coming said another mouse

a young mouse spoke up saying if we tye a bell to the cat its tinkling will tell us when he is near

briliant exclaimed the first mouse

the mice all nodded there heads in agreement a speech was made congratulating the young mice on his plan just as the meeting was about to brake up an old mouse who had been silent spoke

all of youse seem very happy with this idea he said the only thing i want to no is, which one of us is going to put the bell around the cats neck

the mice realized the plans great wekness no matter how clever a plan is, it still has to be possible to cary it out

Corrections

2

1. _____   2. _____
3. _____   4. _____
5. _____   6. _____
7. _____   8. _____
9. _____   10. _____
11. _____   12. _____
13. _____   14. _____
15. _____   16. _____
17. _____   18. _____
19. _____   20. _____

Compound Words

Compound words usually begin as two or more separate words. As they come into common usage together and take on their own identity, they are often written as one word.

For example: finger + nail = fingernail

Usage, rather than set rules, determines the formation of compound words. Some compounds are always written as two words, while others are joined to make a singl e word.

For example: billiard + ball = billiard ball **but** foot + ball = football

Punctuation

The fictional narrative below is made up of 13 sentences. It needs 21 capital letters, 3 commas for nouns in apposition (1 in sentence 1 and 2 in sentence 5), 1 apostrophe, 4 sets of quotation marks, 3 commas associated with direct speech, 1 comma, 12 periods and 1 exclamation point.

1

it had been a hectic day for wealthy business man brett bailey after break fast he had had to rush to a conference in an other city it was late after noon and he was boarding the air plane for the long flight home as he stepped through the door way he saw a familiar face it was his friend jack fitzpatrick who sat reading a news paper

hi jack shouted brett putting down his brief case

with in seconds brett was quickly hand cuffed by three large security guards two police officers drove him down to their head quarters after questioning him they gave him back his watch keys and sun glasses

were very sorry one police officer said as he was putting his flash light away.

yes said an other

i under stand said brett

he went back to the air port and caught the late plane back home

Words

Fifteen compound words have been incorrectly separated. Circle them and write them correctly on the notepad.

2

Compound Words

Sentence 1	_____
Sentence 2	_____ and
	_____
Sentence 3	_____ and
	_____
Sentence 4	_____
Sentence 5	_____
Sentence 6	_____
Sentence 7	_____ and
	_____
Sentence 8	_____
Sentence 9	_____
Sentence 10	_____
Sentence 11	_____
Sentence 12	_____
Sentence 13	_____

3 This story is also a mystery which you can solve. Why did the security guards mistakenly tackle Brett? The answer has something to do with them mistaking two words for a single compound word. Write your answer on the back of this sheet.

Betty Stuart and "Michi"

Punctuation

The factual narrative below is made up of 23 sentences. It needs 58 capital letters, 23 periods, 4 apostrophes showing ownership and 4 commas. It also needs 3 hyphens in sentence 6 and 1 in sentence 17.

Words

The names of people, countries, cities, titles of power and organizations are **proper nouns**. They begin with capital letters. There are 9 different proper nouns in the passage. Highlight them.

There are 14 words that have been used incorrectly. Circle them and write the corrections neatly above each word.

1 Nicknames and slang words are often enclosed in quotation marks. Notice that "Michi," because it is a nickname, is enclosed in quotation marks. Put these in the passage where they have been left out.

---

john kennedy was a former president of the united states of america in 1961 he founded a organization called the peace corps people who volunteer for peace corps duty go to pour countries to work for little money

betty stuart was a nurse who volunteered for the peace corps and was sent to ecuador in south america

in 1976 she was working in a hospital in quito the capital city were she meet a remarkable little girl eighteen month old mercedes michi perugachi came from a very poor family who lived in a one room hut in the andes mountains

her parents were work in the fields when michi went outside to wear the familys pig was tied up somehow she fell into the pigs food bin

when her parents got home they found the toddler lying in a pool of blood the pig had gnawed a way her left arm to above the rist and her right arm close to the elbow

michis parents thought she would never recover they went to look for some white clothes to berry her in

little michi however lived on after three days her parents took her to a doctor in a nearby village the doctor said she had to go to a hospital in quito to have any chance of recovering the

sixty kilometer journey took them two days because they walked most of the way it was in the hospital that betty stuart first met michi her job was to help the little girl recover and lern to live with out hands betty became so attached to the little girl that she asked her parents if she could adopt her and take her back to the usa with her the family agreed and michi grew up under bettys loving cair michi lernt to drive a car and got a job as a telemarketer

the storey of betty stuart and michi is one of great courage it also reminds us what a grate force love is

---

2 In one or two sentences, on the back of this sheet, describe what a telemarketer does.

The Viper Fish

Punctuation

The factual narrative below is made up of 12 sentences.
It requires 12 capital letters and 12 periods. Put them in using different colors.

Note: it's = short for "it is"
          its = "belonging to it"

Words

Each sentence contains an error. Circle each error and write the correction on the line provided. Three apostrophes of ownership are needed.

1

the viper fish is won of the worlds most fearsome-looking creatures if you saw one while swimming you wood probably never go on the water again fortunately, it is unlickely that you will ever see one it patrols the oceans dark botom at great depths sometimes it comes to the surface at nite it never seas the days light the viper fish is well-suited to life on the ocean flore it is black in colore it carrys its own light-emitting organs to help it see in the dark the mouth of the viper fish can open wide enuff to allow it to swallow fish many times its size its stomach stretches to allow it to accommodate large pray with its terrible needle-sharp teeth its a ferocious hunter

2

Corrections

1. _____
2. _____
3. _____
4. _____
5. _____
6. _____
7. _____
8. _____
9. _____
10. _____
11. _____
12. _____

3 Find the verbs listed below in the story. In the space provided, write another word for each that also makes sense.

patrols, sees, carries, swallow, stretches, accommodate

_____

_____

_____

_____

_____

4 **Your Turn**

Write a list of amazing facts about another fearsome sea creature.

Harry de Leyer and Snowman

Punctuation

The factual narrative below is made up of 19 sentences. Put in all the necessary punctuation. Apart from words that begin sentences there are 16 capital letters (note: National Championship). Keep a special lookout for 4 apostrophes of ownership (possession).

1 harry de leyer came from holland he was an expert horseman because of his skill he was able to gain employment as riding master at a private girls school in the united states one day in 1956 he went to a horse auction walking around outside he saw some workhorses they were being loaded into a van to be taken to a slaughterhouse among the sad looking horses harry saw a big grey he like the look of the horse and bought him harrys children called the horse snowman because of the colour of his coat snowman surprised harry when he pit a saddle on the horses back snowman showed a keen interest in jumping harry began a serious training routine with the horse snowman did everything that was asked of him harry decided that the horse was ready for competition he entered him in an important horse show on long island snowman won this competition and went on to win many more the former carthorse won the national championship at madison square garden in new york harrys faith in the apparently doomed horse was rewarded snowman was finally retired to spend his days in peace and quiet

2 "Snowman" is a compound word because it is made up of two words—"snow" and "man." Find four other compound words in the story. List them.

1. _____
2. _____
3. _____
4. _____

3 Write three other words you could add to the word "snow" to make a compound word.

snow_____

_____

_____

Splish and Splash

Punctuation

Each sentence in the narrative below contains two mistakes, not counting capital letters to begin sentences. Put a ring around the mistakes and write the corrections on the lines provided. Put in all punctuation. The last sentence contains four mistakes.

1

splish and splash were too little raindrops _____ _____ there home was a cloud witch floated high above the world _____ _____ the to little raindrops liked to look over the clouds edge and see the world bellow _____ _____ one day they where floating over a verry beautiful place _____ _____ splish and splash leaned over tow far and whent tumbling over the side _____ _____ the little raindrops found themselfs in a farst-flowing stream _____ _____ thay bumped into rocks as the stream pulled them a long _____ _____ it were a relief when the stream ran into a grate river _____ _____ in the river they seen meny unusual things _____ _____ they was afraid when a large silver fish swam bye them _____ _____ after a while they become use to the things that lived in the river _____ _____ they had swiming races whith them _____ _____ suddly the water changed again _____ _____ the river had reached it's mouth and joined the see _____ _____ once again, splish and splash was being tossed a bout _____ _____ the little raindrops looked up and could sea there cloud home overhead _____ _____ splish and splash jumped on a sunbeam and run up it quick _____ _____ they had enjoid there adventure but where glad to be safe in there cloud home _____ _____

2

_____ _____

Listed below are 3 nouns that were described in the story. Use the sentence beginning provided to describe each of them more fully.

(a) a "beautiful place"

It was _____
_____

(b) a "flowing stream"

The stream _____
_____

(c) a "large silver fish"

The fish _____
_____

(d) "cloud home"

It was _____
_____

Answers

Page 9
The Terror of Butter Bay
1. <u>People</u> say a <u>monster</u> lives in <u>Butter Bay</u>. A boy called Bruce swam in the surf one day. Suddenly an arm curled around his *waist*. The water began *to* bubble. Poor Bruce was pulled down. The *farther* he went the more it hurt. He struggled until he was free. *Two* lifeguards *brought* him *to* the *shore*. When his mother *bought* him a new pair of swimming trunks she put them in his *drawer*. He has never *worn* them. He is *too* scared *to* swim in Butter Bay. He says it is not safe. Would you swim *there*?
2. boy, surf, day, arm, waist, water, lifesavers, shore, mother, trunks, drawer

Page 10
Mr. Mullally and His Horse
1. Mr. Mullally <u>owned</u> a shop on the corner of Daisy Street. *Every* morning his horse <u>pulled</u> the cart to market. Mr. Mullally *bought* things there for his shop. He *brought* them back and *placed* them on the shelves before sunrise. Do you *know* what *people* <u>bought</u> at his shop? There were fruits, vegetables, candles, knives, forks, spoons and corks. Mr. Mullally *always* gave his horse a *piece* of apple. The horse *ate* it in a few *seconds*.
2. 1. owned; 2. every; 3. things; 4. placed; 5. people; 6. fruits; 7. always; 8. seconds
3. Teacher check

Page 11
Wise King Solomon
1. <u>King Solomon</u> was a king in <u>Israel</u>. He lived about three thousand years ago. In those days the king was often involved in settling the arguments of ordinary people. One day *two* women came before him. They had both given birth. One of the babies had died. Each woman claimed the baby that had lived was hers. <u>Solomon</u> did not *know which* woman was telling the truth. He said he would ask *one* of his soldiers *to* cut the surviving baby in half. The first woman agreed that this was *fair*. The second woman begged <u>Solomon</u> not *to* do this. She said she would rather the other woman had the baby. <u>Solomon</u> had never intended *to* cut the baby in half. He wanted *to* find out who the real mother was. He *knew*. Do you *know* who the real mother was *too*?
2. Nouns – king, years, days, arguments, people, day, women, woman, witch, soldiers, baby, babies, mother

Page 12
Robin Hood
1. <u>Prince John</u> lived in <u>England</u> *many* years ago. His brother was called <u>Richard</u>. <u>Richard</u> went away to fight a war and <u>John</u> became king. <u>John</u> was a *cruel* king. <u>Robin Hood</u> was a *friend* of <u>Richard</u>. He went *to* <u>Sherwood Forest</u> to get away from <u>John</u>. Other people joined him *here* too. *Two* people who joined <u>Robin</u> *were* <u>Little John</u> and <u>Friar Tuck</u>. While the bad king was on the throne <u>Robin</u> and his men robbed rich people who made *their* money by taxing the *poor*. He gave the money back *to* the *poor* people. <u>Robin</u> was *made* an outlaw. He and his men loved <u>Sherwood Forest</u>. At *night* it was so *quiet* they could *hear* a twig if it fell *to* the ground. <u>Robin</u> and his men stayed *here* until the good king returned. When <u>Richard</u> *came* back he made <u>Robin</u> and his band of outlaws free men.

2. Nouns: brother, war, king, Sherwood Forest, throne, money, outlaw, twig, ground, band
   Verbs: lived, fight, went, joined, robbed, taxing, gave, loved, fell, stayed
3. S1. many; S4. cruel; S5. friend; S13. night; S14. until

Page 13
How to Grow Radishes
1. Radishes are *easy to* grow. <u>They are</u> a very fast growing *vegetable*. You can grow them in most *climates*. <u>They will</u> grow at *any* time *of* the year. The seeds may not germinate in *very* cold regions if you plant them in the middle *of* winter. <u>It is</u> best to plant them in a *rich* soil. The seeds should be planted in rows and watered *regularly*. <u>You will</u> get best results with *your* radishes if you *add* some *compost* to the soil. *They* grow very *quickly*. There are *several* varieties. *Some* are ready for picking in *four* weeks. <u>They are</u> a tasty *addition* to a salad.
2. 1. they're; 2. they'll; 3. it's; 4. you'll; 5. they're
3. 1. easy; 2. vegetable; 3. climates; 4. any; 5. very; 6. rich; 7. regularly; 8. compost; 9. they; 10. several; 11. ready; 12. salad

Page 14
Direct Speech
1. **Rockjaw**
   "I've just been to see a movie called 'Rockjaw,' " said Terry.
   "What was it about?" asked Mavis.
   "It's about a boxer called Rockjaw," replied Terry.
   "Was it good?" asked Raelene.
   "Sensational!" exclaimed Terry.
   The Test
   Mother asked, "Are you reading another 'Goosepimples' book, Colin?"
   Colin answered, "I'm studying for tomorrow's test."
   His little sister shouted, "You are not!"
   "We have to," said Colin in a calm voice, "write a report about our favorite book."

Page 15
Cats and Mice
1. A long time ago cats and mice liked each other. A cat would lift its paw and wave if it saw a mouse. Mice would bow politely when they saw a cat. One morning the King of Cats was walking in the forest. As he was walking his claw became stuck in a hunter's net. He bawled out loudly. Some mice heard him calling. They came quickly.
   "My claw is stuck," he called angrily. "Can you gnaw the string and set me free?" he asked.
   "We are running late for a party on Mrs Squeak's lawn," said one mouse.
   "She makes the nicest strawberry jam," said another, licking his lips hungrily.
   The mice went off. The King of Cats got free but he was very angry. He made a law. If a cat saw a mouse it was its duty to try to catch it. That is why cats and mice are no longer friends.
2. 1. politely; 2. loudly; 3. quickly; 4. angrily; 5. hungrily

Page 16
Ron Mouse's Social Diary
1. On *Monday* I *was* dining at Terry's House of Fine Food. I'd *really* recommend the food there. On *Tuesday* I ran *into* Clint Westwood, Julia Robots and Jim Curry. I didn't *see* the stop *sign*. It was all sorted out down at the police *station*. On *Wednesday* I went to the movies. I saw a film called "People Doing Silly Things to *Each* Other." This is a comedy you *have to* see. It's a *laugh* a second. On *Thursday* I was playing with my poodle in the park. I *picked* up a stick and *threw* it for him to fetch. Just as I looked up I *saw* the basketball *champion* called Jumping Jordon shooting hoops. I went over *there* to *ask* for his autograph. It was when he *picked* me up and stuck me in the hoop I *knew* I'd upset him. On Friday someone came with a *ladder* to get me down. On Saturday I went to the office where it was nice and *quiet* and *wrote* this *column*.
2. 1. Monday; 2. really; 3. Tuesday; 4. sign; 5. station; 6. Wednesday; 7. each; 8. have to; 9. laugh; 10. Thursday; 11. picked; 12. champion; 13. ask; 14. picked; 15. ladder; 16. column
3. Teacher check

Page 17
Rainbow Valley
1. Rainbow Valley is a *colorful* place. Tourists go *there* and marvel at the *unusual* things. They see *pink* elephants *wander* down the *well-lit* streets. People there have *green* dogs. Cats can be *any* color except *white*. *White* cats are caught in the winter when they can be *easily* seen in the *black* snow. *They* are taken to the *pretty* village called *White Cat Town*. The *purple* people living there are proud of the valley. They have *gray* hair. Rainbow Valley has *beautiful* gardens and each house has a *rich* lawn of *blue* grass. The mayor is a *pleasant happy* man. We were *there* on a *recent* visit and he was opening a *new* building. Suddenly the *green* sky turned *yellow*. It *began* to rain huge drops of *delicious* red jelly.
2. 1. colorful; 2. unusual; 3. pink, well-lit; 4. green; 5. white; 6. white, black; 7. pretty; 8. purple; 9. gray; 10. beautiful, rich, blue; 11. pleasant, happy; 12. recent, new; 13. green, yellow; 14. huge, delicious, red

Page 18
Book Review
1. I've just finished reading a ~~very~~ unique book. *It's* called "Strange *Tales*" and is written by Ron Mouse. The book is full of ~~true~~ facts. It can *teach* you a *lot*. *My* favorite *tale* in the book is called <u>"Silent Night."</u> *R*on tells how he fell *asleep* when he *was* at the South Pole and woke up *beside* a polar bear. Imagine that! *Besides* being very interesting it has *some* wonderful *pictures*. Ron *himself* is in most of them. This is Ron's second book. His other book tells of his adventures in the *desert*. Of both the *two* books I think this is the *best*. The book is quite expensive because *its* cover is made of yak leather. *It's* the sort of book you'd be pleased to *lie* down with and read or *lay* on *your* coffee table ~~near the mantelpiece under the moose antlers on the wall~~ to impress the neighbors. What more can I say? Go out and *buy* a copy now!
2. Polar bears are not found in the Southern Hemisphere.

Page 19
Rats and Mice
1. Rats and mice can be found in all parts of the *world*. People have been trying to protect *themselves* from these small mammals since history was first recorded. They are mentioned in writings from *Ancient* Egypt.

Answers

Getting rid of them is not an easy *task*. Some *female* rats can have up to eighty young in a year. Like cats, *their enemies*, rats land on *their* feet when they fall. They can *survive* a fall of twenty meters without being injured. Rats have been known to *tread* water for seventy-two hours.

Rats and mice find people's houses *comfortable*. They eat most foods that we *like*. They *spread* such diseases as plague, typhus and salmonella. You've all seen a cat scraping *its nails* on wood. *It's* doing this to *keep* them from growing too long. Rats and mice, their partners in crime, have the same problem with their *teeth*. They *have to* chew on things to keep them the right length. Sometimes they cause fires by chewing on *electric* wires.

Rats and mice have been *known* as "lapdogs of the *devil*." Can you *understand* why?

Corrections – world, themselves, Ancient, task, female, enemies, survive, tread, comfortable, like, spread, nails, keep, teeth, have to, electric, devil, understand

Page 20
Greyfriars Bobby
1. John Gray was a policeman. He lived in Scotland's capital city, Edinburgh. John's dog, Bobby, loved him very much. Bobby was a little Skye terrier. He used to accompany John on his patrols. John died and was buried in the yard of Greyfriar's Church. For fourteen years Bobby, his faithful friend, stayed by his master's grave. What a loving friend he was! Edinburgh's people came to love the little dog. They made sure he always had enough to eat. Bobby died in 1872. A statue of John Gray's faithful friend was made. It still stands today.
2. 1. rope trick; 2. onion; 3. dressing; 4. stew; 5. chop suey; 6. devil; 7. measles; 8. cheese; 9. toast; 10. checkers

Page 21
1. "Our *captain* killed him in the battle on board *The Pearl*," said the old sailor to his amazed listeners.

    "Teach *wasn't* finished though," he went on. "His body *swam* around the ship seven times before disappearing."

    He was talking about his part in ending Edward Teach's *reign* of terror. Teach was a *pirate*. He was a *giant* of a man with long, untidy hair and a huge black beard. He was *known* as "Blackbeard." When his ship attacked another he *would* put gunpowder and fuses in his hair and set them alight. His victims *must have* thought they were being attacked by a ship from hell. Teach's treatment of those he captured *would have* done nothing to change their minds. He *threw* those he captured overboard in the middle of the ocean. In 1718, Captain Robert Maynard came *after* Teach in his ship, *The Pearl*. He *led* a surprise attack in which the pirate leader was killed. Maynard claimed a *reward* of $200 for stopping Teach's acts of piracy. He *argued* in court for four years. The government argued that the reward was only payable if Teach was *caught* alive. In the end Maynard was paid just $6 and each of his *crewmen* was given $3.

Page 22
Kogi's Dream
1. Topic sentences—italicized
   Transitional sentences—underlined

   Kogi, a priest, lived in Japan over a thousand years ago. He loved to paint pictures of trees, flowers, birds and animals. <u>He liked painting pictures of fish most of all.</u>

   He was painting a picture of a fish one day and began to feel sick. He went to his bed to **lie** down. Two young priests, Kiochi and Hidesato, came to visit him. Kogi did not move. They thought he was dead. Kogi's body was **laid** on a bed in the temple. <u>Kiochi and Hidesato, his two young pupils, sat by the body for three days.</u>

   *On the **fourth** morning they were shocked to see Kogi open **his** eyes.* He told them that he had been turned into a fish. In the water he saw some food on the line. He ate it and felt himself being pulled out of the water. <u>He found himself in the boat of his friend, Bunshi.</u>

   Bunshi, a fisherman, sold him to Juro. <u>Kogi said that he had woken in the temple just as Juro's knife came down on him.</u>

   *The two young priests ran **straight** to Juro's house.* Juro and his family **were** just sitting down to eat a large fish that he had **bought** from Bunshi.

Page 23
Lard of the Flies
   SCENE: The local dump.
   BH (shouting): Brian Blowfly, I've got good news!
   BB (looking up): Hurry up! I've got a date with a doll at Mr. Brown's bin.
   BH (excitedly): This is big.
   BB (becoming annoyed): Get to the point!
   BH: You know that old bookshop on the corner?
   BB: You mean old Mr. Winkle's place?
   BH: That's the one. They're pulling it down and putting up a fast food place.
   BB: Wow, some free grease!
   BH: No more five-kilometer flights to the dump.
   BB: I'll miss old Mr. Winkle a bit.
   BH: I won't. He rolled up a copy of the Saturday Evening Pest and splattered my cousin with it last week.
   BB: That's bad!
   BH: It's not so bad, none of my family liked him much.
   BB: Thanks for the tip.
   BH: Don't mention it.
   (They buzz off stage.)

Page 24
Raiko and the Goblin
1. Raiko *was* a rich man. He lived in Japan hundreds of years *ago*. Even *though* he was rich, he wasn't happy. Every minute *of* his day was spent worrying about his money. He worried that someone would steal it *from* him. High above Raiko's village was a *mountain*. On that mountain *there* lived a goblin. He *wasn't* happy with what he *saw*. He saw Raiko sitting *alone* in his counting house. He could read Raiko's thoughts as he *sat* counting his money. Raiko had a plan to *save* himself money. Years earlier his father had *built* beautiful gardens. They *were* his way of thanking the people of the village. His planning and *their* hard work had made him a rich man. Raiko had *decided* to dismiss the gardeners. The gardens

brought him no money, so why should he pay men to look after them? As he made these plans Raiko *began* to feel sick. He *lay* on his bed and groaned. All of a *sudden* he saw an old priest standing nearby.

"What do you want?" *asked* Raiko.

The stranger answered, "I want you to take better care of the people of *your* village".

Raiko was *enraged*. He picked up a dagger and *threw* it at the stranger. The old priest jumped *aside*. Raiko could not *believe* what he saw next. The old man in the doorway had turned into a huge *spider*. Two of Raiko's gardeners came running when they *heard* his screams. They *chased* the monster to a cave in the mountain. It stopped and said, 'Tell your master to *use* his money to help the poor villagers'. Raiko thanked them when they *returned*. Raiko *spent* half of his fortune to help the poor villagers. To his surprise, although he had less money, Raiko was much happier. When the goblin looked down on the valley and saw the happy villagers it made him happy *too*.

Page 25
Writing Letters
1. Teacher check
2. your, Friday, I've, removed, suppose, really
3. Teacher check
4. newspaper, I'm, tired, week, subscription, were

Page 26
Sammy Cox
1. Sammy Cox's father loved *to* go hunting.
2. He *was killed* in a hunting *accident* when Sammy was still very young.
3. Sammy's *uncle* took care of the young boy.
4. In 1789 he took Sammy on a *whaling* trip.
5. They made the long trip from *England* to Tasmania.
6. The sailors on the ship *liked* playing tricks on the sixteen-year-old boy.
7. They said his uncle *was going* to abandon him on a *deserted* island.
8. These *stories* frightened young Sammy.
9. He *hid* in the bush.
10. He was so afraid he didn't come out of hiding when his uncle and the crew *called* for him.
11. When they weren't able to find him, they thought he must *have* had a dreadful accident.
12. They sailed away leaving poor Sammy behind.
13. Sammy made *friends* with the local Aboriginal people.
14. He lived *among* them until 1806.
15. In that year, an English settlement *began* in Launceston.
16. Sammy worked for a *family* called Cox.
17. He even took on *their* name.
18. When he died, in 1891, he was 118 years of *age*.
19. Sammy *had* lived humbly all of his life.
20. When he died, however, it *was found* that his uncle *had* been a very rich man.
21. Sammy *had been* the missing *heir* to his fortune.

Page 27
Factory Farming
1. The world's *population* is growing rapidly. There are more people than at any other time in *history*. All of *these* people have to be fed. People have developed very efficient ways to *grow* food.

Answers

Some people say that some of the methods used are *cruel*. Should they be *outlawed*? What do *you* think? Do you like *eating* chicken?
In Australia, most hens *are* raised in huge sheds. This is *called* battery farming. Hens raised in these sheds may spend their *whole* lives inside. They only have a small space in which to move. Some hen's cages have *sloping* wire floors. The floors slope so the eggs can roll down to be *collected*. This type of farming *reduces* the price of chicken products. Would you pay $1.00 for an *egg*? Some *people* say chickens get used to living in these cages. People must decide *whether* they are for battery farming or against it. There is a way to stop this method *of* farming. Don't *buy* things grown on battery farms.

2. (a) "When do we eat, Bill?" asked the hungry cowboys.
   (b) "That girl," called Colin, " is my sister."
   (c) Did you place that egg on the table?
   (d) Last night some people, still in their pyjamas, were evacuated from a burning building by firemen.
   (e) The pigs he raised were fatter than those of his father.

Page 28
More Direct Speech

1. F.R. Spofforth (1853–1926) was an Australian cricketer. He was a fast bowler. He had the nickname the "Demon." Spofforth played for club sides in England when he wasn't representing Australia in test matches. On one occasion he was unhappy after some catches were dropped off his bowling. F. R .D. Monroe was his team-mate. He told the 'Demon' to cheer up.
   "In Australia," he said, "even your wonderful Australians missed some catches off your bowling."
   "Never!" exclaimed Spofforth. "I coached them."
   "What did you do?" asked Monroe.
   He answered, "In the part of Australia that I come from we've got hedgerows."
   "Go on," said Monroe.
   "On Sundays I used to take a packet of stones from my pocket," said Spofforth.
   "Then what?" asked the Englishman.
   "I walked on one side of the hedges and they walked on the other," continued Spofforth.
   "How did you improve their catching?" asked his curious friend.
   "I threw the stones into the hedges and they caught the sparrows as they came out," said the "Demon."

Page 29
Good King Wenceslaus

1. King Wenceslaus (903–935) was King of Bohemia over a thousand years ago. Bohemia was part of the country we now *know* as the Czech Republic. Wenceslaus had a twin brother called Boleslaus. *Their* mother, Drahomira, was a pagan. Wenceslaus was *brought* up by his grandmother, Ludmilla. She was a Christian. Drahomira, the *two* boys' mother, *brought* Boleslaus up as a pagan. She hated Christians and had Ludmilla killed. Wenceslaus gathered an army and *fought* the pagans. He won a *great* battle. His soldiers said that they *saw two angels* looking over Wenceslaus during the

conflict. Wenceslaus' mother asked him to come to the city of Bunzlau to have *peace* talks. When he arrived Boleslaus, his pagan brother, murdered him. The people of Bohemia *were* horrified by what had *taken* place and turned to Christianity. Boleslaus repented and *became* a Christian. He had Wenceslaus' body buried in the capital city, Prague.

2. Feast of St. Stephen

Page 30
The Eat-A-Bug Cookbook

1. Are you *tired* of the same old thing? Do you long for the taste of something really *different*? David George Gordon, a U.S. *author*, has written a book that my help you. *Its title* is "The Eat-A-Bug Cookbook." In the book *there* are *recipes* which include such treats as spiders, ants, centipedes, silkworms and grasshoppers. In an *interview*, Gordon said after people have a bite they are *usually* surprised.
   "The Bible," he said, "tells us that John the Baptist lived on a diet of locusts and *honey*."
   "Louis Armstrong, a famous musician, drank a mixture made of boiled *cockroaches* to cure a *sore* throat," Gordon says.
   "I like to point out that *everything* has a reason for being."
   Other *sources* report that tarantulas taste like crab. To cook them, *their* legs are *tied* back before *they're thrown* on hot coals. Termites are *very* rich in *iron*.
   I *wonder* how long it will be before people are *buying* them at the local grocery store. *Perhaps* it will be sooner than you think.

2. tired, different, author, title, recipes, usually, honey, cockroaches, everything, report, thrown, very, buying, perhaps

Page 31
Belling the Cat

1. The mice of a certain household *were* going *through* difficult times. Mr. and Mrs. Roseworthy's cat had *died* and they'd *bought* a new one. For the last years the old cat hadn't *worried* them very much.
   The new cat, however, was a *terror* to the mouse population. He'd only been *there* for a week and had caught ten mice *already*. *Something* had to be done *quickly*. They decided to *hold* a meeting to discuss the problem.
   "My brothers," said one of *their* leaders, "this house isn't a *safe* place for mice since the old cat died."
   Another *joined* in saying, "We have to do something before we are wiped out."
   "The problem is," said the first mouse, " that we can not *hear* the cat because he sneaks up so quietly."
   "We need to find some way to *warn* us he is coming," said another mouse.
   A young mouse spoke up *saying*, "If we tie a bell to the cat *its* tinkling will tell us when he is near."
   "*Brilliant*!" exclaimed the first mouse.
   The mice nodded *their* heads in agreement.
   A speech was made congratulating the young *mouse* on his plan. Just as the meeting was about to *break* up an old mouse, who had been silent, spoke.
   "All of *you* seem very happy with this idea," he said. "The only thing I want to *know* is which one of us is going to put the bell around the cat's

neck."
The mice realized the plan's great *weakness*. No matter how clever a plan is, it still has to be possible to *carry* it out.

2. 1. through; 2. died; 3. worried; 4. terror; 5. there; 6. something; 7. hold; 8. their; 9. joined; 10. hear; 11. warn; 12. tie; 13. brilliant; 14. their; 15. mouse; 16. break; 17. you; 18. know; 19. weakness; 20. carry

Page 32
The Case of the Compound Word that Wasn't

1. It had been a hectic day for wealthy *businessman*, Brett Bailey. After *breakfast* he had had to rush to a conference in *another* city. It was late *afternoon* and he was boarding the *airplane* for the long flight home.
   As he stepped through the *doorway* he saw a familiar face. It was his friend, Jack Fitzpatrick, who sat reading a *newspaper*.
   "Hi Jack!" shouted Brett, putting down his *briefcase*.
   Within seconds, Brett was quickly *handcuffed* by three large security guards. Two police officers drove him down to their *headquarters*. After questioning him they gave him back his watch, keys and *sunglasses*.
   "We're very sorry," said one police officer as he was putting his *flashlight* away.
   "Yes," said *another*.
   "I *understand*," said Brett.
   He went back to the *airport* and caught the late plane back home.

2. S1. businessman
   S2. breakfast, another
   S3. afternoon, aeroplane
   S4. doorway
   S5. newspaper
   S6. briefcase
   S7. within, handcuffed
   S8. headquarters
   S9. sunglasses
   S10. flashlight
   S11. another
   S12. understand
   S13. airport

3. Hi Jack! (hijack)

Page 33
Betty Stuart and "Michi"

1. John Kennedy was a former President of the United States of America. In 1961 he founded *an* organization called the *Peace Corps*. People who volunteer for Peace Corps duty *go to poor* countries to work for little money.
   Betty Stuart was a nurse who volunteered for the Peace Corps and was sent to Ecuador in South America.
   In 1976 she was working in a hospital in Quito, the capital city, *where* she *met* a remarkable little girl. Eighteen-month-old Mercedes "Michi" Perugachi came from a very poor family who lived in a one-room hut in the Andes Mountains.
   Her parents were *working* in the fields when Michi went outside to *where* the family's pig was tied up. Somehow she fell into the pig's food bin.
   When her parents got home they found the toddler lying in a pool of blood. The pig had gnawed *away* her left arm to above the *wrist* and her right to close to the elbow.
   Michi's parents thought she would never recover. They went to look for some white clothes to *bury* her in.
   Little Michi, however, lived on. After three days her parents took her to a doctor in a nearby

Answers

village. The doctor said she had to go to a hospital in Quito to have any chance of recovery. The sixty-kilometer journey took them two days because they walked most of the way.

It was in hospital that Betty Stuart first met Michi. Her job was to help the little girl recover and *learn* to live without hands. Betty became so attached to the little girl that she asked her parents if she could adopt her and take her back to the U.S.A. with her. The family agreed and Michi grew up under Betty's loving *care*. Michi *learned* to drive a car and got a job as a telemarketer. The *story* of Betty Stuart and Michi is one of great courage. It also reminds us what a *great* force love is.

Proper Nouns – John Kennedy, President of the United States of America, Peace Corps, Betty Stuart, Ecuador, South America, Quito, Mercedes, Michi, Perugachi, Andes Mountains

2. telemarketing – the selling of goods or services by contacting potential customers on the telephone.

Page 34

The Viper Fish

1. The viper fish is *one* of the world's most fearsome-looking creatures. If you saw one while swimming you *would* probably never go in the water again. Fortunately, it is *unlikely* that you will ever see one. It patrols the ocean's dark *bottom* at great depths. Sometimes it comes to the surface at *night*. It never *sees* the day's light. The viper fish is well-suited to life on the ocean *floor*. It is black in *color*. It *carries* its own light-emitting organs to help it see in the dark. The mouth of the viper fish can open wide *enough* to allow it to swallow fish many times its size. Its stomach stretches to allow it to accommodate large *prey*. With its terrible needle-sharp teeth *it's* a ferocious hunter.

2. 1. one; 2. would; 3. unlikely; 4. bottom; 5. night; 6. sees; 7. floor; 8. color; 9. carries; 10. enough; 11. prey; 12. it's

Page 35

Harry de Leyer

1. Harry de Leyer came from Holland. He was an expert horseman. Because of his skill he was able to gain imployment as riding master at a private girls' school in the United States. One day in 1956 he went to a horse auction. Walking around outside he saw some workhorses. They were being loaded into a van to be taken to a slaughterhouse. Among the sad-looking horses Harry saw a big grey. He liked the look of the horse and bought him. Harry's chldren called the horse Snowman because of the color of his coat. Snowman surprised Harry when he put a saddle on the horse's back. Snowman showed a keen Interest in jumping. Harry began a serious training routine with the horse. Snowman did everything that was asked of him. Harry decided that the horse was ready for competition. He entered him in an important horse show on Long Island. Snowman won this competition and went on to win many more. The former carthorse won the National Championship at Madison Square Garden in New York. Harry's faith in the apparently doomed horse was rewarded. Snowman was finally retired to spend his days in peace and quiet.

Page 36

Splish and Splash

1. Splish and Splash were *two little raindrops. Their* home was a cloud *which* floated high above the world. The *two* little raindrops liked to look over the cloud's edge and see the world *below*. One day they *were* floating over a *very* beautiful place. Splish and Splash leaned over *too* far and *went* tumbling over the side. The little raindrops found *themselves* in a *fast*-flowing stream. *They* bumped into rocks as the stream pulled them *along*. It *was* a relief when the stream ran into a *great* river. In the river they *saw many* unusual things. They *were* afraid when a large silver fish swam *by* them. After a while they *became used* to the things that lived in the river. They had *swimming* races *with* them. *Suddenly* the water changed *again*. The river had reached *its* mouth and joined the *sea*. Once again, Splish and Splash *were* being tossed *about*. The little raindrops looked up and could *see their* cloud home overhead. Splish and Splash jumped on a sunbeam and *ran* up it *quickly*. They had *enjoyed their* adventure but *were* glad to be safe in *their* cloud home.